To: V.

God Bless you and
I look forward to
spending time with you!

Inspirational Love

[signature]
9/30/01
770-745-5235

Published By:
Poetic Writes
P.O. Box 1000 • Austell, Georgia 30168
(770) 394-2605

Copyright ©1999 by Andrea L. Mills

All rights reserved.
No part of this publication may be reproduced, stored in or introduced into retrieval system or transmitted, in any form, or by any means (electronic, mechanical, photocopying, recording or otherwise), without the written permission of the author.

Edited by: Kirk L. Haynes • Donna M. Jones

Photography • Stanley & Tammy Howard

Layout and Design by:
Custom Made For You
graphic design studio
P.O. Box 956986 • Duluth, Georgia 30095
(770) 923-8783

ISBN: 0-9672832-0-5

inspirational love

DEDICATION

This book is dedicated to my family with a special thanks to my Mom and Dad. There were many times I depended on you all to brighten my day, encourage me, and keep me focused on the prize. I thank each of you for always being there to listen to my poetry and share my dreams. Your strength and love throughout my life has inspired me to write "Inspirational Love." I will always be grateful to you, my family.

TABLE OF CONTENTS

INSPIRATION

If	2
Amazing Grace	3
And All Just For Me	4
Faith	5
God's Sufficient Grace	6
Hold On	7
He Is First	8
When God Appeared To Me	9
In A Flash	10
In The Beginning	11
In Time	12
Everything Must Change	13
No More Than He Will Allow	14
Silent Prayer	15
They That Wait	16
Tomorrow	17
I Believe In Me	18
Friendship	19
Victory • A Cancer Survivor's Poem	20
You Will Win • A Healing Prayer	21
Dreams	22
Every Day People	23
I Am Here For You	24
I Can	25
Special Friend	26
Thank You	27
The Gift	28
Yesterday	29
You Lift Me Up	30
Lady	31
Celebration	32
A Million Men	33
The Woman That I Am	34
The Old Man	35
No Other	36
Mom And Dad	37

inspirational love

My Sisters • Lucinda, Vickie, Theresa and Mary 38
Before You Go • A Mother's Prayer................................39
A Father's Love..40
If Not For You 41
If I Could - Especially For Naqwanda Ramsey....................42
I Remember Belton • In Memory of Belton Rocks 43
Believing 44
Dr. King, We Owe You 45

LOVE

Groove Me 47
Last Night 48
It's You...49
Precious Memories 50
How Many Times 51
For Always 52
As I Lay..53
A Well Dressed Man 54
Dreams Of My Man 55
Color Me Bad 56
Forever...57
Forgive Me 58
Have I Told You 59
I Know..60
Meant To Be...61
Sand To The Beach 62
Say It..63
The One 64
The Question 65
The Answer 66
What I Need...67
The Things That I Like Most About A Man 69
Annie's Swing..70

inspirational love

inspirational love

Foreward

It has been said that a dream is a wish your heart makes. Needless to say, my heart is happy today as this dream comes true for me. The book, "Inspirational Love," is about family and friends sharing their hearts and thoughts with others in search of better relationships and closer family ties.

I have compiled some of my most precious poetry to share with you. Many of the poems have been written just as they were given to me through spiritual enlightenment. Through writing and sharing poetry with others, I have learned that God wants the best for all of us. It is my hope that my book will encourage you to be strong, follow your dreams, and share God's most precious gifts with those who are most important to you.

"To God Be The Glory For The Things He Has Done"

-Andrea L. Mills

inspirational love

Inspiration

inspirational love

IF

If I told you I had plans, Would you know what
I had in mind? If I told you I needed your help,
Would you clear your schedule to find some time?

If I told you I was going to be great and have it
all one day, Would you encourage me with hope
or would you find discouraging things to say?

Well, all of these things I tell you and it's with
determination I must strive, Because these dreams
are my biggest plans and they help to keep me alive.

They will one day feed my family and buy beautiful
gifts for friends, They will remain my connection
to God because it is he who grants all things.

So the next time someone tells you that they have
hopes and dreams, Tell them just how proud you are
no matter how hard it seems.

Through you a person can gain courage to stick with
the hardest fight, But remember that he who counts
how long knows it didn't happen over night.

Amazing Grace

Amazing Grace is my song and I can tell you why, It will always be my song of praise until the day I die.

To know that by Grace I was saved, Yes, a wretch like me, Jesus paid it all upon the cross He set me free.

I once was lost upon this earth, no home could I find, But Grace came along and picked me up just in the nick of time.

When danger appeared and blocked my way, clouding my heavenly view, Grace was there to take my hand and it was Grace that brought me through.

Amazing Grace is my song and I will forever sing the praise, Because God's wonders never cease to always leave me amazed.

I can't imagine my life or any other without the Grace, It runs throughout my body and I wear it upon my face.

So, should you hear my song, know that God is in the place, And you too have been saved by His "Amazing Grace."

And All Just For Me

There is nothing more precious to me than a man laying down his life, As a sacrifice for another, willing to pay the price.

Well, this is what Jesus did and He did it all just for me, So my soul would not be lost, He died to set me free.

Nailed to the cross, Jesus hung His head and died, In pain but not alone, you see there were many that day who cried.

But on the third day from His tomb, Jesus was up and gone, Witnessed by believers someone had rolled away the stone.

And still to this day we speak of the miracle that took place, Thanking God for His son and His saving Grace.

I know I can never repay the Savior for the gift of eternal life, But I can live my life righteously surrounded by spiritual light.

No, I can never repay the Savior because He died to set me free, But I can say, "Thank You, Jesus," Because He did it all just for me.

FAITH

Through all of my trials and despairing cries I've learned to hold my head up high, I know that I am not alone because my God is standing by.

Day after day I have repeated my prayers waiting on the answers they might bring, You see faith is substance of things hoped for and the evidence of things not seen.

God will do what He said He will do but you must have faith to wait and see, But there is no joy like the joy I've found in knowing that what God has for me is for me.

Hold on to God's unchanging hand and believe that your faith will see you through, His rod and His staff will provide comfort but keeping the faith is up to you.

God's Sufficient Grace

God's Grace is Sufficient and it's always enough for me, It's just enough light in darkness to provide a way for me to see.

At times life clouds my way, leaving me confused by the ups and downs, But then God's Grace steps right in making everything just fine.

Sufficient Grace is what God gives each of us today, You see Jesus died a long time ago and it's because of Him that we're all saved.

God, The Father, will do as He promised if only we do His will, Follow his Commandments, walk in His spirit and be willing to forgive.

God's Grace is Sufficient and He wants all of His children to know, That we are never ever alone, For He is with us everywhere we go.

So if you are looking for everlasting life, step out on your faith, You will never know anything more perfect than God's Sufficient Grace.

Hold On

If the days drag on with no end in sight, And the nights appear cold without the trace of light.

If you've come to the point of disappointment and despair, Hold on to your dreams there's help out there.

Out in the distance, far away from you, A watchful eye has everything in view.

All that you want and all that you will gain, Is soon on the way because everything must change.

Just hold on fast to the moment at hand, Nothing just happens it's all in God's plan.

Soon you will see that all of this will pass, Hold on a little longer because trouble don't last.

He Is First

God created heaven and earth and all to
Him I owe, He blesses every step I take
and He is with me wherever I go.

He takes His time to care for me each and
every day, He calms the storms in my life
and quietly leads the way.

He loved the world so much that He gave
His only son, Now we have a right to life
and our battles are already won.

I often try to fight for myself knowing the
battle is not mine, Then God shows up to
save the day and He is always right on time.

God is first and loves us all as we are saved
by His Grace, And He shall reward those who
believe in Him and keep the faith.

WHEN GOD APPEARED TO ME
(Inspired by Emogene Brookins Lewis)

One night I had a dream and God appeared to me, He shared with me His vision and it was as clear as it could be.

I asked Him for love, peace, and happiness to share with each of you, Watching the trouble in this world, it was all that I could do.

He showed me what I asked and like magic He painted the scene, And as I stood next to Him, He revealed it on a screen.

God said, "I am love and I love within your soul, I will bear for you your burdens and be with you wherever you go."

The sun beams as happiness and is there to light your way, It will guide your path and bring you happiness each and every day.

But peace was most inspiring because it comes in the calm of night, you can find it in the sky surrounded by little twinkling lights.

The moon is your peace, my child, and peace will lead you through, It will calm your spirit and give you rest as it makes you feel brand new.

So know that I am always with you and one day I will come again, But my love, my happiness, and my peace are with you until then.

In A Flash

My life flashed before me and in an instant it was gone,
there was nothing left of me and no need to carry on.

The life had been removed and the spirit it was dead,
there were no beautiful places floating around in my head.

All I saw was darkness and it scared me to the bone,
just to think that my wonderful life was suddenly all gone.

When I awoke I realized it had all been a dream, then I
looked to the sky to ask God what did it mean?

The answer that I got was to rethink my life and
never to give up on anything at least not without a fight.

For God's peace, love, and joy I'm thankful everyday, And
taking my life for granted is certainly not the way.

The answer that I got was to take nothing very light, God
had me in mind when He made the sacrifice.

Giving His only son so that my life would have a meaning,
and it would be a shame to waste this gift without ever seeing.

That it could all be gone, all within a flash, with the answers
never given because I didn't ask.

So Lord, I ask for a second chance without reliving the past, I
would hate for my life to be over and gone in a flash.

IN THE BEGINNING

When God created the heavens
He did it all alone, Then He
created me and you and you
thought He did something wrong.

Black and white together is how
He intended it to be,
I was to respect you and you
were to respect me.

But somewhere down the line
things got out of hand,
Black became secondary
to the white man.

My brothers and my sisters, Black
and white the same,
We have got to stand together
to be separate is a shame.

We are all intelligent people with
the minds of Kings and Queens,
If we work together I know we
can accomplish anything.

Just remember that in the beginning
God created heaven and earth,
Black or white it doesn't matter
because none of us were first.

In Time

In every life some rain must fall and the clouds will hide the sun, Trials will come on every hand and victory will seem little to none.

But don't give up and never give in and please don't ever quit, It has been proven that in times like these the harder you push the stronger you get.

Often times the race is lost for those who lack the faith to win, You know that the race is never given to the swift but to those who endure till the end.

Yes, Life is funny with its twists and turns and endless roads of twine, But don't give up and never give in because victory will come "In Time."

EVERYTHING MUST CHANGE
A Man's Prayer for Change

Many things around me changed and I find that I did too, Because I no longer enjoy the things that I used to do.

Life is very short and leaves no time for childish games, It's all about making the most of the time that remains.

Because God is coming back, He told us that He would, And He will surely separate the bad from the good.

So I'm about the Father's plan now that I'm a man, Boyish things fell away when I began to understand.

That God is truly wonderful and He has plans in store for me, I'm living my life as a Christian Man because I intend to see,

My Savior when He comes and removes me from this place, And I'll say, "Thank You Jesus," When I meet Him face to face.

No More Than He Will Allow

God is truly wonderful, marvelous in every way,
He builds a shield around me each and every day.
No one has the pleasure of pulling me up to knock
me down, Because they can never do more than
the Father will allow.

I went to Him for protection and He gave me a shield,
He gave me His instruction book and it tells me how
to live. With it comes peace like a river flowing mild
because no one can do more than
the Father will allow.

Yes, God is here for me and He is also there for you,
Should you ever need him here's what you should do.
Call on Him today and know that He is listening
now, and believe that no one can do more than
the Father will allow.

Silent Prayer

Today I prayed a Silent Prayer and I know that I was heard, Because of God's compassion for me, I believe He listened to each word.

My request was very simple, The prayer wasn't just for me, It was for all of those who feel the pain and need to be set free.

Set free from the struggle of barely making ends meet, Set free from the feeling of being denied a peaceful sigh of relief.

Set free from the feeling that hope won't ever be restored, And set free from blaming others because they feel they've been ignored.

My Silent Prayer was prayed for everyone in the world today, But especially for those who are hoping and praying for a brand new day.

I know that God heard me and He won't ever let us down, So don't forget to thank Him when He turns your life around.

They That Wait

Many times in life we often forget that the Lord wants us to wait, Getting in a hurry won't rush a thing because God decides your fate.

He has an ultimate plan for your life and struggle may be His will, You must have patience to wait on Him and in time your pain will heal.

It's God's time that matters most and not yours when He decides, He controls the wind and the rain, but you must trust Him and abide.

God is very kind and He has many blessings already planned, Learn to put your trust in God and not in the foolish words of man.

He will lift you up to fly with the eagles as they soar high above, Wait on the Lord and pray for strength and He'll surround you with His love.

They that wait upon the Lord shall renew their strength, And until your blessing comes to you pray without ceasing and be content.

Tomorrow

What would you do if it all went away?
The dream for tomorrow would only be today.

No time for planning, wishing or hoping;
No tomorrow in sight only today and then nothing.

What would you do if it all went away?
Maybe your dream for tomorrow should begin today.

There is still time for praying, dreaming, and giving;
Just don't wait until tomorrow before you start living.

I Believe In Me

I've made excuses along the way
but I can hardly count them all,
I guess disappointment comes a dime
a dozen and as many as tears that fall.

Yes, I believe in me and it is now
time for me to take a stand, Because
I know that all of my dreams can come
true but I need to lend a hand.

My hands can build, my hands can hold,
and they can write from A to Z, I can
achieve anything that I dream because
my dreams will allow me to be free.

So today I'm taking an extra step to
become the person I dream to be,
And I will not stop until I succeed
because "I Believe In Me."

FRIENDSHIP

Every once in a while people come along and
they steal your heart away, By doing nice
things and being there, they always
brighten your day.

You do this for me and I am so blessed
because I can call you friend, If I had to list
the wonderful things you do, my list
would never end.

So, I thought I would tell you just how special
you are and it comes from my heart, I know
that we will be friends for life and I will let
nothing tear us apart.

If ever the time should come around and
you need a friend to care, Please know that
you can always count on me and Yes, I will
be there.

Thanks for always sharing your smile
as you spread your joy around, Friends are
jewels planted deep in the earth and you are
the best that I have found.

VICTORY
A Cancer Survivor's Poem

If you thought I couldn't make it,
Just look at me now.
If you thought I couldn't take it,
then you are still asking how.

If you ask me how I beat it then
you already know the odds,
But the answer to your question
is still in the hands of God.

It took me to understand that
things happen for a reason,
All of us have our days and
they don't rotate like the seasons.

But when your day comes along, I
pray you have someone there,
There is nothing like a bowl of soup
and a dose of friendly prayer.

So, for those of you who have beat
the sickness that cancer brings,
Raise your hands up high and believe
that God can do anything.

And for those of you who have yet
to learn about cancer and it's fear,
Remember that people really care
and for you we'll be right here.

YOU WILL WIN
A HEALING PRAYER

The thought of winning and coming in first is only where you start, The ending is made when you have the desire to achieve what's in your heart.

The race is never given to the swift but to those who endure till the end, So keep your faith and look ahead because today you stand among friends.

Think back for a moment on yesterday when things weren't going your way, But like the winner you truly are, you kept striving for a brighter day.

And look at you now fighting for your life and the dreams you hold on to, Not one of us here can feel your pain but we are here to help you through.

God only knows when a cure will be found but we know it is soon to come, We must continue to praise His name and thank Him for all He has done.

When things get tuff, you can lean on me but don't you ever bend, Keep fighting the battle and you will see that through the joys of life "You Will Win."

DREAMS

Dreams are made of concepts that
are visions in the mind, But you
are what makes them happen
through the faith that you find.

But faith isn't just lying around
because it lives within your heart,
It's what keeps reality in check
with hope from the start.

A thousand times you have seen it
and you know what lies ahead, It's
the drive to keep going when you
could have stopped instead.

Yet your dreams will keep you
yearning for the feeling of success.
The same feeling a bird must feel
upon first flight away from the nest.

Anyone can dream but a dreamer
continues on, Because the world
will tear you down to make sure
that you are strong.

Dreams are all you have when the
picture comes into view, No one
else has control but faith will see
you through.

Reality will show it's head to make
sure that you have hope, then the
dream will keep you strong while
walking upon the rope.

So never give up on any dream
but if you do, just start again;
With a little faith and touch of
hope reality will share your win.

Every Day People

Some people want life easy but don't care to pay the price, Nothing is easy and trouble is free but that's a fact of life.

What you get out is what you put in and you get nothing more, Yet some will go through life hoping to even up the score.

The fact is... You'll meet many people while traveling your road of fate, You won't succeed all the time so remember that it's never too late.

You can always try again and make something special of your world, Even an oyster can see the beauty in a grain of sand before the pearl.

God created each of us to share our special gift, So never look down on any man because tomorrow you may need a lift.

Work hard to find your moment as you respect others along the way, Count your blessings, say your prayers and thank God for every day.

I Am Here For You

I am here for you if you need me
to help you through your pain,
I know that you are wishing
that all things were the same.

But things change for reasons and
most times we don't know why,
But trust in God and know that
we'll understand by and by.

Just know that I am here for you
to talk or just hold hands,
Lending my ear to comfort you
and to help you understand.

These words won't bring back the
link that is now missing in your life,
But they will tell you I'm here for
you as your friend and your wife.

I Can

Although they were just two small words
you said to me one day, Those words
meant more to me than I could ever say.

The words were spoken kindly and
they allowed me to strengthen my
mind, Far beyond any reality and right
into another time.

A time of success and change, a place
where I'm in charge of me,
Following my dreams and in control,
up front for all to see.

Those words won't be forgotten, just
remember they came from you,
Because you said, "I Can",
now others will know it too.

SPECIAL FRIEND

Sometimes we have to stop and thank our special friends, For always being wonderful through the thick and thin.

I don't care to imagine you not being there, To talk with, laugh with or maybe just to share.

You have been there for me so many times before, And I wanted to tell you that you're too special to ignore.

So if you ever wonder how much you mean to me, Spread your heart around the world then maybe you could see.

That your friendship is priceless and for all that it's worth, I would never trade it for anything on this earth.

THANK YOU

It's nice to know that people care
when you can see it in what they do,
And because of what you did for me
I wanted to say thanks to you.

God puts people in place for us and
we must continue to do His will,
Because only then can we step out
on faith to see His promises fulfilled.

May God forever bless you and be
the light that leads your way,
And I will always be thankful for
the time you brightened my day.

THE GIFT

Talent comes in many forms, as many as
shades of light, And if you are in search of
yours, keep searching both day and night.

Never stop short of finding your gift because
there is one given especially to you,
Through this gift you can do wonders and
in the process make dreams come true.

Friends, family, loved ones, and admirers
will all tell you how great you are, But
only your confidence and sincere devotion
will make you shine like the brightest star.

YESTERDAY

Yesterday wasn't long ago, it was just the other day, The one I hoped for, the one I longed for, and the one I wasted away.

I saw it coming and in my sorrows did nothing to prepare, I sat around feeling sorry for myself and I didn't see the need for prayer.

How could I not thank the Lord for this beautiful day He gave to me, How ungrateful, and selfish, and unthankful could I be.

But God is very kind and He has given me another day, This one I will treat differently and it won't be treated like yesterday.

Today I am going to thank God for all the things He has given to me, I especially want to thank Him for His son who died to set me free.

You Lift Me Up

Whenever I am feeling down, it is always you who lifts me up, Somehow you make me take note of the fullness of my cup.

It's then I realize what a blessing life can be, Many of us are truly blessed but we never look around us to see.

God has answered many prayers, some that we didn't even ask, But He gave it as a blessing for serving the least and the last.

"Whatever is asked in my name", the Father said to us, Then we only have to step out on faith and fill our hearts with trust.

Thank you, my friend, for always being there to lift me up, I only wish everyone knew the fullness of their cups.

LADY

Lady, What makes you think that I have nothing else to do, But run around here cleaning things all of them just for you.

Yes, I know you're tired but Lady, so am I. Remember I saw you take a nap and I haven't shut an eye.

Do you know that when I finish here my husband needs me too, My children will have to hold my feet while I untie my shoe.

Yes Lady, I need this job I can't do nothing else, No one thought that I could read just cook and dust your shelves.

You know one day I'll tell Lady and I'll tell her just like that, Maybe I'll do it tomorrow as soon as I come back.

CELEBRATION

History is about looking back to see from whence you've come, To reflect on where you are going and to take pride in what you've done.

We as a people are celebrating the progress we have made, As memories always come back to us to remind us of the days.

When our grandmothers and grandfathers told us stories around the fire, When they picked cotton in the fields and their families were for hire.

Times of disappointment but also times of joy, When they expanded their families with the birth of a girl or boy.

Days of watching and waiting for word to travel down hill, To be told that they were free by the signing of a bill.

Wait no longer my people because the celebration has begun, But there is still work to do and races to be won.

Black History is about your life and by reflection we all can survive, Because as long as we look back we can never forget to strive.

A MILLION MEN

They came together one day from every walk of life, Dedicated to a cause with minds made up to fight.

Not for the wrong but for the right in which they believed, A new dawning of the day when the black man is really free.

Free to stand up for each other, their families, and their friends. No time like the present, this is where it should begin.

At the capital of a nation built with strong hands, putting a mark upon history, this one for the black man.

For black men have given so much to build this country strong, So how could anyone think this movement to be wrong.

Yes a million men, standing together black and as proud as they could be, I was glad that I was watching because it was truly something to see.

The Woman That I Am

The woman that I am is the one I've worked hard to be, Knowing nothing would come easy and nothing is priced free.

The woman that I am has learned to hold her head up high, With a positive attitude letting nothing pass her by.

The woman that I am takes care of the home, Quick to stand by her man so that he knows he's not alone.

And If you should ever notice the way I walk into a room, I leave nothing for you to guess and very little to assume.

Every woman should be proud to make her presence known, For we are only here for a little while and then time moves on.

Let the woman you are speak for you like only you can, Then you too can say you have become the "Woman That I Am."

THE OLD MAN

I know the old man standing under the light
for I have talked to him on many nights.

His wisdom is great and his knowledge is high,
he knows the answers when I ask why.

I know the old man walking behind the mule, he had
to walk through days when there was no school.

He had to work to do his family proud; Keeping silent
his tears trying not to cry out loud.

I know the old man asleep in the chair, I have watched
him with the greatest of care.

When he is asleep it is something to see, his snores
sound like waves crashing rocks on the sea.

I know the old man I speak of above and since
I was a child he has shown me love.

He hasn't changed much and for that I am glad, In
case you didn't know he is my dad.

No Other

Mother, I want to tell you what you are to me,
The strongest woman on this earth, through
the years I've come to see.

You have endured it all without ever looking
back, Leading the way for your children to follow
in your tracks.

Providing all that was needed to keep the family
strong, Turning mistakes into lessons learned when
we did something wrong.

Making use of every dime to help meet every
end, And I never would have known it because
you kept it within.

I never went without, You wouldn't hear of that,
Because you held me high upon the highest
throne I sat.

And when it was time to leave and go out to live
alone, You always let me know that I could come
back home.

For these things I say, "Thank You," You are the
greatest mother, If asked who else would have
done it, I'd proudly say, "No Other".

MOM AND DAD
(Written Especially For Eva and David Mills)

How can I ever repay you for
the love you've shown to me,
For turning on the light when
in darkness I couldn't see.

For giving of yourselves and
doing more than parents should,
And for always being there
because you said you would.

Well, Should the day roll around
when you need me to be there,
Should you ever have a doubt
about how much I really care.

Should you ever reach for me
to give you a helping hand,
And should you ever need an
anchor while sinking in the sand.

Know that I'll be here because
I love you both so much,
My heart is open wide just
because of your loving touch.

You have given of yourselves
and for this I am so glad,
I thank God for the gift
of calling you Mom and Dad.

MY SISTERS
(Lucinda, Vickie, Theresa, and Mary)

Since the day that I was born
I have always had the four of
you. You share my joy, and feel
my pain as we do what sisters do.

I love each of you with all my
heart and I thank God all over
again. No one can ever compare
to you, My sisters and my friends.
          I Love You

BEFORE YOU GO
(A mother's prayer for college)

I've always been around to remind you of what to do, Clean the dishes, straighten your room and even to tie your shoe.

But now that you are leaving, going to college to fill your mind, I would like to remind you of what you are leaving behind.

A mother who loves you dearly, one who wishes she could be there, To help you through the troubled times always to show she cares.

One who would take on your battle to be number one in your class, One who would jump at the chance to keep watch through an hour glass.

To watch you as you grow and do the best you can, Changes will take place in time and you will learn to understand.

Understand the right and wrong that is awaiting at the door, Behind it many challenges, some you have never faced before.

I know you can do it, I've prepared you as best I could, I've been ready for this moment since the time of motherhood.

Remember the things I've taught you when the answers you just don't know, I simply wanted to remind you one more time "Before You Go."

A Father's Love

A Father's love is special as it shapes
the life of his kids, When they grow up they
will say thanks for all the things that you did.

It's nice to know they can count on you whenever
they need you there, Because a father keeps a
family strong when he shows them that he cares.

Every child should celebrate their father's
love because when he's gone it will mean much
more, And each father should remember that
he is the one his kids adore.

If Not For You

Mother, I want to say thank you
for the many things you've done,
And for always being supportive
because your love compares to none.

Growing up wasn't always easy but
you made it better by being there, You
have always given me the best of you
and I know how much you care.

You are a wonderful mother and a
special lady too, And it's a blessing
to know for me that there is nothing
you wouldn't do.

You have never failed to show your love
and help me to find my way, You
told me to always believe in God and
and you taught me how to pray.

Thank you Mother, for believing in me
And helping to make my dreams come
true, I have no idea where I would be
today, If it had not been for you.

IF I COULD
(Written Especially For Naqwanda Ramsey)

If I could just remember your smile when things aren't going right, If I could just remember your courage when I feel that I've lost the fight.

And if I could just remember your strength when I feel mine cannot be found, Then I could only realize what a hero you are right now.

You have always given me great joy and I am so proud of you today, And thankful that God heard my cry when all I could do was pray.

Today is your day and I am glad you did your very best, Always trying to reach your goals and never stopping at nothing less.

So know that I am very happy because you have done real good, This is the day that the Lord has made and I wouldn't change it "If I Could."

I Remember Belton
(Written In Loving Memory Of Belton S. Rooks)

I remember Belton, His smile could light
the room, But no one ever imagined that he
would be leaving us so soon.

I remember Belton, He would do anything,
All you had to do was ask and as a friend
he would jump right in.

And I remember Belton so full of life and
love, I know that having him here with us
was a gift from God above.

So please always remember Belton and if
you knew him I can bet, That he is a man
that all who knew will surely never forget.

BELIEVING

Believing in love is so easy from the very start, The feelings of the soul somehow over rule the heart. But then there comes a time when it falls into place, You know it's just not right from the look on each others face.

Believing then tells you that things will be all right, Yet you find yourself alone day after day, night after night. People say things will get better and you believe for just a while, But suddenly hope brings no laughter and laughter brings no smile.

So then you pick up your pieces, The other half is gone, You find yourself in pity, saddened and alone. But this is where believing pulls you back to your feet, Telling you there is no failure and you won't fall to defeat.

Believing is a joy that one finds inside, No one gave it, No one takes it, It has always been your guide. Believing says be strong, Tomorrow is yet to come, Live your life to the fullest depending on no one.

Believe in yourself, It is you who deserves the most, Hold up the champagne glass and give yourself a toast. Believing is something that never leaves you alone, God keeps us believing by reminding us to be strong. Believing is just doing it and the gate is open wide, Head out to life, make the move, God is on your side.

Dr. King, We Owe You

Dr. King we owe you a world of thanks, for
dedicating your life to positive change and
giving all that it would take.

You were fighting for people who were treated
unfairly from the very start, Being judged by the
color of our skin and clearly not by our hearts.

For the hearts of those strong and pure, you were
dedicated and steadfast, For black people you gave
everything to reach freedom at last.

Today and each day we thank you for your
sacrifice, And Dr. King, you gave the most
because in the end you gave your life.

Your life was put on the line so we could make
it to the mountain top, We must still remember
to climb because the struggle hasn't stopped.

Now we celebrate a day in your honor and
be it forever true, King Celebration Day
is just a mere token of what we owe to you.

Love

GROOVE ME

Have you ever met a man that was just bad
to the bone? Whenever we're together I
pray he never leaves me alone.

Girl, the brother Grooves me like nothing
I've ever known. It's more than just a feeling
cause when he lifts me he's so strong.

Groove me, baby I said, and he knows just
what to do. Why if you could see what
he's giving me, I know you'd wish it were you.

Groove me baby, Groove me, I said just one
more time. And he said I'll always groove
you if you say that you'll be mine.

So Girl I said yes, I couldn't let him slip away.
I couldn't imagine another woman saying the
things that I now say.

And I'm holding on to my man forever and
a day, And as long as he continues to Groove
me, I'll always feel this way.

So ladies, If you find a man to groove you, Hold
on tight for dear life. And if you are as smart as
me, You too may become his wife.

LAST NIGHT

Last night I had a dream and it was a good one indeed, You were all the man I desired and you were all the man I'd need.

I slipped out of my attire and slowly wrapped in your arms, I felt so good and wonderful there, I was totally safe and warm.

After closely lying next to you my body began to melt, And every woman who has ever had a dream knows exactly what I felt.

My body was into yours and yours was into me, It was enough to curl my body up although I was fast asleep.

Yes, last night was a good night and I slept through without a break, Just to remember how real it was makes my knees slightly shake.

Today I hope to have the nerve to share my thoughts with you, Because I can think of nothing better than having last night come true.

It's You

Sometimes I stop to give thanks for the love that we share, It's nice to know that you understand me and that you really care.

The day that we became one was the happiest day of my life, And still I can think of nothing more precious than us becoming man and wife.

I promise to always be there for you and I will never leave your side, Just to hear your voice on the telephone still makes me smile with pride.

Yes, I am proud to be with you and I want the world to know, That I am your lover and your friend and I will never let you go.

You have given me great joy and I must admit it's true, There was one person made for me and I am happy to say, "It's You."

Precious Memories

You came into my life at a time that I call right, I couldn't believe my life had changed and I wasn't alone each night.

You are still my closest friend and my only one true love, You brought with you the peace of God and He blessed us from above.

Your smile still lights my way when there is darkness all around, And sometimes I feel your heart beat when I focus on the sound.

Our life together was wonderful before God called you home, But He left with me your presence so I will never be alone.

I thank God for this blessing that He gave to me through you, You will always be a precious gem with a light shining through.

Our precious memories comfort me and help me through each day, And as long as I can remember your smile I know I'll be okay.

How Many Times

How many times have you dreamed
about me before falling asleep at night,
How many times have you heated the
oil before allowing it to sooth my back.

How many times have you thought about
the pleasure of kissing me from head to toe,
How many times have you fantasized about
just how far I would go.

How many times have you stirred the bubbles
that will soon form around my breast, How
many times have you gone under to explore
the places beneath my chest.

How many times have we made love before
being interrupted by the dawn, And just how
many times have our bodies joined in the
midst of a quiet storm.

Well, for all of those times and so many
more, I have also dreamed about you,
Holding, kissing, touching, and teasing
while doing the things that lovers do.

It's nice to know I'm not alone and that
dreams can be entwined, I simply wanted to
ask you my brother, "Just How Many Times."

FOR ALWAYS

I come to you this moment to dedicate my heart
and soul, And I want to make a pledge to love
you until the day that we grow old.

I promise to be your best friend, your lover,
and your guide, I'll take care of you with
everything I have and I'll do it all with pride.

Today I become you as you dedicate yourself
to become me, Together we will climb the
mountain top to soar as the wind sets us free.

I have dreamed of this very day since I
was a little child, Hoping and praying for
someone just like you all the while.

You have done so much for me and I plan to give
even more to you, You are my lover, and best
friend and you help to make dreams come true.

So let today be forever side by side the rest of
our days, And may we never forget the promise
to love each other for always.

As I Lay

After you left me last night, I Just laid
quiet for a while, I wanted to take a moment
just to remember your sweet smile.

Your gentleness will forever be a memory in
my mind, In case I never see you again
and this was our last time.

I wanted to tell you I loved you but I didn't
want to scare you away, So I decided to keep
it in and tell you some other day.

Why is it that I'm afraid to let my feelings
show, If I don't ever tell you then I guess
you'll never know.

But for now the thought of loving you tonight
will have to do, As I lay quiet a little longer
to think about me and you.

A Well Dressed Man

There is something about a man in a suit
that really turns me on, To see a suit is to
touch a suit. Ladies, correct me if I'm wrong.

When we see a man in a suit we just assume
he's got the flow, We don't really care if he
does or not and don't really care to know.

It's that suit, it's that man, it's that look he
gives when I pass, It's his body, it's his hair,
and did I mention his ...

Ask me what he does, this well dressed man,
I couldn't tell you but he's got my attention
and right now I'm his biggest fan.

Yes, It's that suit, it's that man, together on
the street, Hand in pocket, shoulders straight,
and he doesn't miss a beat.

It's that suit, it's that man, standing over there
beside my chair, Think about it ladies, you've
had the dreams, we have all been there.

So men, go to your closet and find the suit,
you know that one that catches her eye, And
if at first it doesn't work then at least you
know you've tried.

You have nothing to loose, so take my advice
if you can, I'm trying to tell you there's
something about "A Well Dressed Man."

Dreams Of My Man

Do you ever stop to dream of your man and
the things you want in life, Sometimes I get
carried away with the thoughts of being his wife.

What I want most from my man is not found just
any where, I have dreamed about having a man
with compassion and a sensitive side to care.

I want to be gently touched on my shoulders
by hands that feel just right, The same hands that
will caress my body and hold me tight each night.

A man who will always share with me and from
across the room show his loving smile, A man who
would do anything to care for his wife and child.

This man will promise to love me always and pledge
to do it all again, And when we grow old we'll both
know for years that we've always been best friends.

For me these thoughts were more than a dream when
they all came true, I got my man and thanks to my
dreams I already knew just what he would do.

COLOR ME BAD

What's wrong with my color? It's a question
that's oh so sad, Because when I look around
I see black men have colored me bad.

Black men don't seem to notice how beautiful
we are, By we I mean the black women who
are not white by far.

It seems that black men want women who vary
in skin tone, And everyone is simply leaving the
black woman alone.

Well, I'm here to say I've noticed and white men
just aren't my fad, But black men you find white
women and then you color me bad.

Don't get me wrong, I like God's people too, But
I'm tired of looking in my mirror thinking;
Girl, What's wrong with you?

My brothers you can help if you would remember
the struggles we've had, Years and years of hearing
that black was so bad.

If you cross the line, Do me a favor and try not
to brag, Because now I realize it wasn't my
color, Just your thinking gone bad.

FOREVER

Forever is the time that I want to
be with you, Forever is the love
that makes our marriage true.

Forever is the time that you can
count on me, Forever is the spirit
that makes our joy run free.

Forever is the day our hearts
will meet above, Together
even then to share this sacred
love.

So think of us as forever and keep
this thought in mind, Forever is
together until the end of time.

Forgive Me

Sometimes in life we say things without knowing the reasons why, It may not dawn that we've said the wrong things until others start to cry.

Whether you keep your tears inside or they stream down for all to see, I just know that I caused you pain and your tears are because of me.

Let me say that I was wrong and I never meant to break your heart, If only we could communicate to each other the way we did from the very start.

Yet somehow we have lost the gift to keep our relationship true, We forgot that it wouldn't be an easy task but it was work we were both willing to do.

Because I promised to love you gently and give all of me to you, You then promised to lay next to me and let your love flow through and through.

Baby, If in your heart you can forgive me it would be a special moment in my life, As we try to recapture the love we once shared by starting with tonight.

HAVE I TOLD YOU

Have I told you lately that I love you? Well, I'm happy to say I do, you have changed my life by bringing me joy as you help to make my dreams come true.

And never could I have imagined a love that would grow this strong, It's nice to know that you are my man and that I will never ever be alone.

Nothing is ever too much for you because you never mind going out of your way, Just knowing that someone loves me this much somehow always brightens my day.

We love each other completely and that is all I can ask of you, And I know that you are giving me your all because you make me feel brand new.

I will be here with you always, right up until the end of time, You're the best thing to ever happen to me and I'm so glad to know you are mine.

You make me laugh, you make me smile and I get excited whenever we touch, You caress my body, tickle my fancy, and you give me a little rush.

I will always be here because for me you were there and all I am is because you, And If I haven't told you lately that I love you, please know in your heart that I do.

I Know

Often times I open my eyes just to
watch you as you sleep, Carefully
observing your very presence and
the things that make you unique.

Your face so handsome and so kind
with a gentle and subtle smile, Your
black body so beautiful, sexy, and
sleek and for that I would walk a mile.

Your chest, a monument of your great
stature is firm yet oh so smooth, Yes
I'm in heaven whenever we touch just
before I slip into my groove.

How could I forget your sculptured
waist as I hold on to melt into you.
Sex so good that you wish you could
stay forever with nothing else to do.

I've watched you close and touched
your body all while you were asleep,
And ladies let me tell you that the rumor
is true, always observe the hands and feet.

But it's all of these things that make up
my man and he is bad from head to toe,
You see I watch him whenever he is
asleep and I assure you that's how I know.

Meant To Be

All of my life I prayed for someone who would love me for me, And now every day that I look at you I know that we were meant to be.

Through the trials of life you found me and I am blessed that I found you, I could never ever find another man who has done for me what you do.

I pray that you will carry my love in your heart wherever you go, And know that I love you so much that I wanted to let you know.

Nothing will ever change inside no matter what changes I go through, No matter how many things change, I know there will never be another you.

Each time you look at me I pray that you too will see, That nothing will ever come between our love because we were "Meant To Be."

SAND TO THE BEACH

Now, why would I bring sand
to the beach? All of these men
standing within my reach.

I can pick and choose and do what
ever I please, I can look around and
make my choice from one of these.

You will never catch me bringing
sand to the beach, If someone is at
my side then I'll never be able to
creep.

Go searching, go looking or just
venture out and seek, This is why
I'll never bring sand to the beach!

SAY IT

Turn off the lights and light the fire because I've been waiting for you, I've got the desire to feel your body while doing the things that lovers do.

Oh I've had a hard day but it won't compare to the hard I have in mind, You can bet after the first all you will hear from me is baby do it to me one more time.

And after that is through don't be surprised if I ask you for a little bit more, Tonight is the night and I've got plans for you like never before.

I'm gonna take my time and erase the line that keeps us from doing new things, After tonight you won't forget because our love will forever be changed.

So close your eyes and feel my thighs as they wait for you to stake claim, The fun won't stop until my body gets hot and I hear you shouting my name.

THE ONE

Woman when I tell you I love you, You need to know that I'm for real. This is not just another line but rather something that I feel.

I know sometimes you may hear the same story from other men, But they don't know who I am and they can't tell you where I've been.

I've been looking for a woman, both independent and strong, And I want you to know that I am here to help you fix whatever is wrong.

When you become tired of all the troubles that others have given to you, Come and rest your head on my shoulders until the sun lights the morning view.

Yes woman, I am the man that you have been afraid to give a single chance, But I'm not afraid because you're the one for me and I knew after taking one glance.

THE QUESTION

Hello Lady, I was just admiring you and noticed
you were sitting here alone. I wanted to take
just a moment to let you know you've got it
going on.

Your hair and dress both look really great
and I can tell that you are fine, In fact when
you walked through the door I thought man, I
wish she were mine.

No, this is not a standard line, I wouldn't
say it if it weren't true, I would give anything
for a chance with someone that looks like you.

Let me tell you a little bit about myself
because I am an honest Man, I have a
mission in life and you, my lady, can be part
of my plan.

Yes, I have a car, a house and I enjoy sailing
on my boat, Need I say that they are all mine,
you see I paid off the monthly note.

I work hard everyday and let me tell you
it's the only way I know, I paid my own way
through college because I saw the need to go.

So if you have a moment, I am asking for some
time, If it's okay , I'd like to have a seat
and buy you a glass of wine.

The Answer

My, My, What a coincidence this
night has really turned out to be,
I mean me admiring you while you
were admiring me.

When you walked through the door,
I thought, Now I like his style, And
you could have sold me for a penny
after I saw your beautiful smile.

You know I don't usually like or
enjoy the club scene, It never
represents real life when you
awake from last nights dream.

But I wanted to meet a classy guy
so I decided to step out, I felt I
would meet my match tonight;
in fact I had no doubt.

Your life sounds very interesting
and I would like to hear more, It's
wonderful to meet successful men
because needy ones can be a bore.

Yes, I would enjoy talking with you
now that you have asked me for
some time, And as far as my drink,
White Zinfandel suites me just fine.

inspirational love

What I Need

I don't need a man to prove to me
that he's big and strong, And I don't
need a man to roll me over expecting
to do me all night long.

I don't need a man hanging around
just to tell me what to do, And I don't
need him to stick to me as if bonded by
super glue.

I don't need him to be jealous when
others look at me, I don't need him to
get upset if I go out on a shopping spree.

I don't need him to turn his back
when he gets all uptight, And I don't
need him to pull away if I want a kiss
good night.

But if you ask me what I need I'll gladly
share with you, What I need when it
comes to a man from my point of view.

I need my man to comfort me whenever I'm feeling down, I need my man to support me when my strength cannct be found.

I need my man to think that I am beautiful inside, I need my man to walk with me showing love and pride.

I need my man to confide in me no matter what may be going on, I need him to share his feelings when he feels all hope is gone.

I need my man to love me with all he has to give, I need my man to have compassion and be willing to forgive.

This may seem like too much if you don't care to understand, But these are the things a real women needs when it comes down to her man.

The Things That I Like Most About A Man

The things that I have grown to like
most about a man, Are the things in life
I've come to know I will never understand.

Like how he makes me smile at almost any
time of day, And the way he might forget the
answer but know just what to say.

And the way I slip into his arms, a perfect
fit at most, or the way he does it to me
to make me melt like butter on toast.

Or the way he holds his hand out to help
me along my way, Or how he holds my body
tight whenever he wants to play.

Or perhaps the way he holds his tears as if
to keep them in, Or the way he slowly wipes
them away as they trickle down his chin.

Or how he stops to admire my beauty and
sends a special spark, Or how I feel like
he shot an arrow and aimed it for my heart.

Yes, these are the things that I like most
about a man, And as long as I am happy
who cares if I understand.

Annie's Swing

Beautiful Lady, come and swing with me just
one last time before you go, The last time I
would ever swing with you but how was I
to know.

Seeing your smile dance across the room
that night is a vison I'll always see, And
it's your loving and warm embrace that
keeps your spirit here with me.

We talked that night before the dance and
as always I listened real hard, Some of the
stories I had heard before but still I gave an
approving nod.

The things you told me won't ever go away
and your memory will live on, I will continue
to cherish my time with you and Al Green
will keep singing your song.

Thanks for leaving your treasures with me
because you were truly a Royal Queen, I will
forever be thankful to God above for
allowing me one last swing.

ORDER FORM

Name: _____
Address: _____
City, State, Zip: _____
Telephone: (_____) _____

Item	Qty	Price	Total
PORTFOLIO POEM	____	$18.00	_____

    11 x 14 Matted Poem
    Poem(s) can be personalized to your specifications
    See Table of Contents for Poem Selection

SPECIAL OCCASION   ____   *   _____
    11 x 14 Matted Poem
    Written especially for you.
    You supply the thought and consider it done!
    *Call for Quote

DESK POEMS   ____ $15.00   _____
    5 x 7 Matted Poem

INSPIRATIONAL LOVE   ____ $15.00   _____
    A Collection of Poetry

BOOK MARKS   ____   2@$5.00/   _____
    Choose your Favorite Poem $3.00 ea.

For orders of $20.00 or less, please add $4.00 for shipping and handling. For orders in excess of $20.00, please call for shipping and handling charges.

Mail Check to:
Poetic Writes • P.O. Box 1000 • Austell, Georgia 30168
(770) 394-2605

inspirational love